COMMODORE JOHN BARRY

From the painting by Gilbert Stuart. By permission of Mrs. W. Horace Hepburn, of
Philadelphia, Grand-niece of Commodore Barry

COMMODORE JOHN BARRY

THE FATHER OF THE AMERICAN NAVY

A SURVEY OF
EXTRAORDINARY EPISODES
IN HIS NAVAL CAREER

BY

WILLIAM BARRY MEANY, M.D.

HARPER & BROTHERS PUBLISHERS
NEW YORK AND LONDON
MCMXI

ILLUSTRATIONS

COMMODORE JOHN BARRY

The Father of the American Navy

Beneath his guidance, lo! a navy springs,
An infant navy spreads its canvas wings.

ONE of the finest types in the entire history of the American navy is Commodore John Barry, the first Captain placed in
command of the first war-vessel commissioned
to fight under the Continental flag—the *Lexington*, named after the first battle on land in
the Revolution: and it was Barry who captured in battle the first British war-vessel,
and thus achieved the honor of having the
first British flag struck to him in naval battle,
in the struggle for independence under authority of the Continental Congress.

The indomitable courage, devotion to duty,
and successful achievements which character-

ized the entire career of Commodore Barry, his splendid naval and military record as a soldier, won for him the admiration of friends and foes —and require no emphasis or embellishment by eulogistic remarks; a patriot without reproach, one who loved his country, so that in serving it he wanted no recompense—a grateful nation should mete out the act of tardy justice, so long delayed, to Commodore John Barry, in a way of befitting honor to the memory of the Father of the American navy, and a great patriot in the early destinies of our country—so that his memory will live until the end of time:

> His glory nothing lacks,
> But ours lacks him.

SIGNS NON-IMPORTATION ACT

Without illumination I propose for the moment to direct attention to the early part taken by John Barry in the cause of liberty and independence. We find among the signers of the Non-Importation Resolves the name of John Barry, a ship-master of Philadelphia, actively engaged in the mercantile marine mainly to and from South Amer-

ican and West Indian ports until 1774, when
he made voyages in the *Black Prince*, the
finest, largest, and fastest of the American
commercial fleet, sailing from Philadelphia to
British ports. He took an active part in the
early movements of the colonies for liberty
and independence.

Affairs of the colonies were becoming more
and more strained with England. A congress
of the colonies met at Philadelphia. The
Non-Importation Resolves (which Barry sub-
scribed to and signed) were set forth in
the Articles of Association entered into in
1770 by the gentlemen of the house of bur-
gesses and the body of merchants assembled
in Williamsburg, Fairfax County, Colony of
Virginia, in opposition to taxes imposed by
England to raise revenue upon the people of
the colony. They contain a number of
clauses (resolves): one, against the purchasing of English goods, etc.; another to stop the
further importation of slaves and to suppress
those slave-traders who were engaged in that
nefarious traffic. (See reprints on file in the
manuscript rooms of the Congressional Li-
brary at Washington, D. C.)

BARRY OFFERS SHIP AND SERVICE

While Barry was in London with his ship, the *Black Prince*, much history was being made—and observing the trend of events, he, in September, 1775, hastily returned to Philadelphia. He arrived home on October 13, the very day Congress resolved to fit out two armed cruisers, one of fourteen guns, the other of ten guns. Barry at once offered his ship and services to Congress, which were accepted. His business affairs then were at the height of their prosperity, but his sympathies were so strongly and fervently with the cause of the colonies that he sacrificed his fortune and private interests and at once enlisted in the Continental navy.

BARRY'S RANK THAT OF SENIOR

From that day, October 13, 1775, to the end of his eventful career (by death) September 13, 1803, John Barry was the senior or ranking officer of his ship and squadrons, and at no time did he serve under the orders of a senior officer, reporting direct to Washington, Congress, or to the secret and marine committees.

4

COMMODORE JOHN BARRY

LIVES IN HISTORY

The history that accompanies the data hereinafter to be given is taken from the Continental and United States Congressional Records; official and private letters of Washington, Robert Morris, Franklin, Benjamin Rush, McHenry, Stoddert, and others; papers of the marine and secret committees, and, therefore, is not subject to the distrust that accompanies all accounts of "history" made to order or taken from the memoirs or personal diaries of the actor himself or its direct beneficiaries. Unofficial records are entitled to respect, though like all authority of this nature, their facts should be received with caution.

It would seem meet, then, that measures should at once be taken by the proper governmental authorities for the accurate compilation of the official records of service and characteristics—as evidenced in such records, manuscripts, etc., as are in reach of and now in the possession of the government—of each distinguished officer of the early navy (known, perhaps, to the older officers of the navy, but unknown to the public), and arranged in alphabetical order and in chronological sequence as to be available in print for the use of midshipmen at Annapolis, and for distribution, either free or at a nominal fixed price, for public and semi-public libraries for the correct information of a generous public—so that he who runs may read and he who reads may know.

WASHINGTON'S TRUST IN BARRY

It was befittingly left to our immortal Washington to repose special trust and confidence in Barry's patriotism, valor, and abilities by rapid promotion, as evidenced by executive appointments and high commissions on special, hazardous, and most important voyages—and so recorded by trustworthy and dispassionate commentators, such as James Fenimore Cooper, Dr. Benjamin Rush, Dennie, Preble, Abbot, Frost, Charles A. Dana, George Ripley, and others of high literary attainments — esteemed, respected, and supported by Washington, who attached Barry as his aide-in-chief at the very commencement of hostilities, showing clearly that Barry is justly entitled to the designation of father of the American navy.

HEAD OF WASHINGTON'S FLEET

On October 5, 1775, Washington directed a letter to Congress, with an urgent request to that body for the building, or purchasing and equipping, of two vessels, one of fourteen guns, the other of ten guns, to be placed at his disposal and under his orders, etc.

On October 13, 1775, Congress, taking into consideration the report of the committee—Deane, Langdon, and Gadsden—appointed to prepare a plan for intercepting vessels coming out with stores and ammunition, after some debate, Resolved: "That two vessels carrying, one fourteen, and the other ten guns, a proportionable number of swivels and men should be fitted out."

This was the commencement of our American navy, and what became known as Washington's fleet. The heavier armed, the *Lexington*, 14 guns, was given to the command of Capt. John Barry. He was appointed captain (the highest rank attainable by authority of the Continental Congress) on December 7, 1775, though selected some time previous to that date by Washington.

7

COMMODORE JOHN BARRY

The proposal of fitting out a fleet to combat the greatest and most powerful sea force of the world, that of Great Britain—said to be of a thousand ships—did, indeed, seem to be to the most resolute defenders aside from Washington, Morris, Barry, Rutledge, and a few others, a foolhardy undertaking, and when Rutledge, of South Carolina, moved the appointment of a committee to prepare a plan and estimate of a fleet, many made the proposition a subject of ridicule.

BARRY SAILS ON "LEXINGTON"

With the *Lexington* Barry put to sea, and with his light brig was enabled to pass through a narrow channel left open and free from heavy ice, the main channel of the then heavily ice-blocked Delaware River at that time being impassable; and in Preble's *Origin of the Flag* it is declared that his (the *Lexington*) "was the first vessel that bore the Continental flag to victory on the ocean."

The incident of raising the first "American flag" on the *Alfred* in the earlier months of 1776 is always related with patriotic glamor, as though the stars and stripes, our national

8

or American flag, was first hoisted by the then Lieut. John Paul Jones, as so often has been stated in public print.

In the *Journals of the Continental Congress*, Vol. 8, the following resolution was adopted on June 14, 1777: Resolved, "That the flag of the United States be thirteen stripes, alternate red and white; that the Union be a blue field, representing a new constellation."

The first mention on the records of the nation presents the name of John Paul Jones to Congress on December 22, 1775, as first on the lists of lieutenants of the new navy reported by the marine committee for confirmation. He was appointed as a lieutenant to the *Alfred*, commanded by Captain Saltonstall. That the gallant Paul Jones served our country well, both as a lieutenant and afterward as a captain in the navy, is undisputed.

THE "LEXINGTON" FIRST REGULAR CRUISER

In the *History of the United States Navy*, by James Fenimore Cooper (himself a midshipman in the navy, attaining the rank of a lieutenant, and acquiring an experience which he found most useful in his literary career), published in 1839, the following appears in Vol. 1: "For the first regular cruise that ever got to sea under the new government we must refer to the *Lexington*, 14 guns, a little brig, the command of which was given to Capt. John Barry, a ship-master of Philadelphia of credit and skill. The honor has long been claimed for Captain Barry, and, on as close examination of the facts as our means will allow, we believe it is his due. The *Lexington* must have left the Capes of the Delaware late in January or early in February, and her orders were to sail southward."

CAPTURES FIRST WAR-SHIP IN BATTLE

"As an offset," writes Cooper, "to the escape of the British ship *Glasgow*, 20 guns, after engaging 'Commodore' Esek Hopkins's squadron, consisting of the *Alfred*, 24 guns; *Columbus*, 20 guns; *Andrea Doria*, 14 guns; *Cabot*, 14 guns and the *Providence*, 12 guns, off the east end of Long Island, on the morning of April 6, 1776, the *Lexington*, Captain Barry, a small brig of 14 guns, fell in with the *Edward*, an armed tender of the *Liverpool*, on April 7, 1776, off the Capes of Virginia, and, after a close and spirited action of nearly an hour, captured her. The *Lexington* had four of her crew killed and wounded, while the *Edward* was cut nearly to pieces and met with a very heavy loss of men."

Barry succeeded in entering Delaware Bay with his prize, though strongly blockaded by British war-ships, and arrived at Philadelphia on April 11, 1776, bringing the news direct to Congress of the first capture of an armed vessel taken in battle, and thus the honor of having the first British flag struck to him by a British war-vessel in battle under Continental authority, and rejoicing the hearts of the patriots so much that even John Adams gleefully wrote: "We begin to make some figure in the navy way." Richard Henry Lee, in a letter describing the event, narrated that the enemy did not submit until he was near sinking.

Frost, in his *Commodores of the Navy*, writes: "In February, 1776, he (Barry) was appointed to the command of the brig *Lexington*, 14 guns. She was the first Continental vessel of war that sailed from the port of Philadelphia."

In the American Cyclopedia, which was projected in 1857 by Charles A. Dana, formerly Assistant Secretary of War (1863–1864), managing editor of the New York *Tribune* (1849–1862), late editor-in-chief and former owner of the New York *Sun* (George Ripley, formerly literary editor of the New York *Tribune* and associate editor with Dana in the American Cyclopedia), appears the following: "At the commencement of the Revolution Barry offered his services to Congress, and in February, 1776, was appointed to command the *Lexington*, 14 guns, and after a sharp action took the tender *Edward*, the first war-vessel captured by a commissioned officer of the navy."

Josiah Bartlett, a signer of the Declaration of Independence, writing to John Langdon, said: "Captain Barry in the *Lexington* has taken and sent in here a privateer of 6 guns, commanded by another of those famous Goodriches, of Virginia." Cæsar Rodney, another signer, wrote on August 3, 1776: "Yesterday came to town an armed vessel taken by Captain Barry at sea."

Henry Fisher, in his report to the committee

of safety of Pennsylvania, wrote: "Last evening the *Kingfisher*, a British man-of-war, returned into our road with a prize brigantine, Captain Walker, of Wilmington, but, luckily for us, our brave Captain Barry had been aboard of her and taken out the powder and arms." It may be well here to state that the records of the secret and safety committees at that time show that the patriots were sadly in need of powder and arms.

Three more vessels were captured by Barry with the *Lexington*, and then upon his return to Philadelphia he took charge as superintendent of the construction of war-ships then building on the Delaware River.

CHEERS HEARTS OF PATRIOTS

These captures and achievements of our infant navy thrilled the patriots to new endeavor, for those first months of the war were, as Thomas Paine wrote of them—"the times that tried men's souls."

"Capt. John Barry, whose spirited action off the Capes of Virginia, in the *Lexington*, 14 guns, has been mentioned," writes Cooper, "and whose capture, April 7, 1776, of the *Edward* on that occasion is worthy of note as having been the first of any vessel of war that was ever made by a regular American cruiser in battle."

Barry's report of this victory embraced a few lines, giving the bare details, and concluding: "I have the happiness to acquaint you that all our people behaved with much courage." Barry was innately modest in regard to his public (naval) and private achievements. He kept a strict account in detail of what he thought were his mistakes—but not of his successes.

ACTIVE SPIRIT OF MARINE COMMITTEE

Barry was the active spirit of the marine committee, and during the next few months remained in and about the Delaware capes under orders "to take, sink, and destroy the enemy's vessels."

Under the direction of Washington and Robert Morris—the latter a signer and the financier of the Revolution—Barry was placed in command (commander-in-chief) of the port of Philadelphia, then the largest mercantile and shipping port of the country.

ATTACKS ENGLAND'S NAVY

Here we take leave of the *Lexington*, the first war-vessel commissioned and given to the command of Capt. John Barry, who, in the dead of night, brought his little brig past the guns of two large British war-ships, then guarding the mouth of the Delaware, going out single-handed "to take, sink, and destroy the enemy's ships," such as merchantmen and armed privateers, and harass and to attack the ships of England's powerful sea force (a British fleet composed of 70 armed vessels then guarding the coast, among which were the *Roebuck*, 44 guns, and the *Isis*, 32 guns, then guarding the mouth of the Delaware River; with the *Pearl*, 32 guns, the *Liverpool*, 28 guns, and the *Augusta* and *Merlin* guarding the capes of Delaware), and, once clear of the shore, he unfurled for the first time under Continental authority that flag "which has ever since floated in triumph over every wave, and never while God is Just will it disappear from the sea that it ruled."

BARRY GIVEN COMMAND OF "EFFINGHAM"

Barry's exploits were rewarded by his appointment to command the *Effingham*, a frigate of 28 guns, then being built under his supervision at Philadelphia. Before her completion she was taken up the Delaware River to escape the British army which then invested Philadelphia, and was afterward destroyed by order of Congress "to prevent it falling into the hands of the British forces," though Barry, with violent emphasis, opposed her destruction, and left no doubt in the minds of the committee of his serious earnestness—and again time proved the correctness of Barry's judgment.

IN ROW-BOATS CAPTURES ARMED SHIPS

Tiring of what he termed inactivity in awaiting to take command of the incompleted *Effingham*, Barry manned four small row-boats, having spied a large schooner mounting 10 guns and flying the British flag, with four armed transports, loaded with provisions and forage for the enemy's forces, lying below Philadelphia, then invested by the British army;

16

he rowed down the river, with muffled oar-locks, passing the guarded river-front of the city during the night and, at early daylight, succeeded in rowing his boats alongside of the armed schooner, and before the English suspected the presence of any enemy, Barry, at the head of his men, was clambering over the rail of the schooner, cutlass and pistol in hand. The astonished Englishmen threw down their arms and rushed below. The victorious Americans battened down the hatches. Barry ordered the soldiers and sailors on the four transports to surrender on penalty of being fired into, and triumphantly, and in sight of a heavily armed British war-ship lying below, carried all five prizes to the piers at Fort Penn, and put the four transports in charge of Captain Middleton, who had command of the fort. Then the hatches were removed, and the American sailors being drawn up in line, Barry ordered the prisoners to come on deck.

It was found that Barry with his twenty-seven (27) American sailors had captured one major, two captains, three lieutenants, and one hundred and thirty armed soldiers, sailors, and marines.

That was the most brilliant feat of arms upon the seas, and it was the most far-reaching in its results. From that moment the British in Philadelphia became insecure. They felt their supplies in danger. Indeed, it hastened the withdrawal of the British forces from Philadelphia.

Frost, in his *Naval Biography*, said of this achievement: "For boldness of design and dexterity of execution it was not surpassed during the war."

SENDS SUPPLIES TO WASHINGTON

Part of the stores were forwarded to General Washington, and the prisoners were turned over to the proper authorities. The heavily armed British war-ship which was lying below in the river having hove in sight, Barry took the captured schooner into shallow water, hoping to save the schooner from being recaptured, but in this he was unsuccessful. Barry succeeded in landing his prisoners with war supplies, and then, firing a shotted cannon down the hatchways of the captured schooner, destroyed her before the British war-ship came up.

WASHINGTON THANKS BARRY

Washington wrote Barry the following letter: "I congratulate you on the success which has crowned your gallantry and address in the late attack upon the enemy's ships. Although the circumstances have prevented you from reaping the full benefit of your conquests, yet there is ample consolation in the degree of glory which you have acquired. You will be pleased to accept my thanks for the good things which you were so polite as to send to me, with my wishes that a suitable recompense may always attend your bravery."

Washington took occasion to publicly thank Barry and his sailors for this extraordinary achievement, etc.

Of this, and similar character of service, Franklin wrote: "Nothing will give us greater weight and importance in the eyes of the commercial world than a conviction that we can annoy on occasion their trade and carry our prizes into safe harbors."

TRANSPORTS WASHINGTON ACROSS DELAWARE

Terror reigned in Philadelphia. Even the great Washington sounded the note of despair. "In ten days," he wrote, "this army will cease to exist. We are at the end of our tether." From New York across New Jersey he was being pursued by Cornwallis. Barry quickly organized a company of volunteers and went to Washington's aid. On that gloomy Christmas eve he rendered valiant aid in transporting Washington and his army across the ice-blocked Delaware, and served with honors and distinction in the victories of Trenton, Princeton, and elsewhere, that again gave heart to the despairing patriots and drove the English back to New York.

BARRY AGAIN FIGHTS ON LAND

Here we find Barry again fighting in the field under Washington. The following is a copy of Washington's letter to Barry:

HEADQUARTERS, *15th April, 1778.*

To Captain John Barry:

SIR,—In a letter received from you some days past were enclosed the paroles of some officers; those I have delivered to the Commissary-General of Prisoners. Yesterday I received the articles agree-

COMMODORE JOHN BARRY

able to the bill sent me by Major Burnet and by
him or when he sends down you shall receive the
amount.

The men at present under your command belonging
to General Varnum's Brigade I cannot think of suf-
fering to remain with you, so long as you perhaps
may wish, and have to desire that you will send
them by a careful officer to camp by the first day
of next month. Their time of stay will be so
short that I cannot think it necessary or right
that they should receive their clothes until they
join their corps.

(Signed)   G. WASHINGTON.

WASHINGTON'S CONFIDENCE IN BARRY

In reply to Cornwallis's request for con-
veyance of relief to the wounded, Washington
gave a signal mark of his confidence in his
selection of Barry as his representative to
secure the safe conduct of the wounded, the
surgeons, medicines, and baggage; and when
that work was completed Barry resumed his
position as commander-in-chief of the port of
Philadelphia, defending it from British invasion by sea, and harassing the enemy and
capturing their vessels of war and merchantmen.

COMMODORE JOHN BARRY

COMMANDER-IN-CHIEF OF PORT

It is pertinent here to call attention to a letter addressed to "The Commander-in-chief John Barry of the port of Philadelphia," signed by twelve navy lieutenants seeking redress for "certain grievances," which Barry transmitted to Congress. (See *Continental Congressional Record*, session, July, 1777.)

IN COMMAND OF BRIG "DELAWARE"

Next we find Barry commanding a "letter of marque," clearing and capturing the enemy's ships then investing the Delaware Bay and River, and here he again gives remarkable exhibition of his fighting qualities. As you are aware, there were two elements controlling the naval forces of the Revolutionary powers at that time. There were the State naval forces and the Continental forces. Barry was now in command of the brig *Delaware* under the State naval forces, and made several important captures; he on one cruise brought into Philadelphia three captured vessels.

COMMAND OF THE "ALLIANCE"

Upon his (Barry's) return to Philadelphia he was designated to command a new ship of 74 guns, but that ship was sent to France, Congress having concluded to present her to the French King, and Barry was assigned to the *Alliance*, the finest and fastest ship in the Continental navy.

CONVEYS COMMISSIONERS TO FRANCE

To secure further aid from France the *Alliance* was ordered to convey our special commissioner, Col. John Laurens, to France. His father, who had also been an envoy, had been captured and was a prisoner in the Tower of London, and great precautions were needed for the safety of our representatives on most important missions.

Accompanying Laurens as passengers upon the *Alliance*, and entrusted to Barry's care, were Thomas Paine and the Count de Noailles. Barry safely landed his passengers in France, and Laurens succeeded in securing from the French King six million livres (gold), and it was this "hard" money that enabled Washington to pay his army, and absolutely necessary to the prosecution of the war—the Continental forces had reached the end of their resources. It was this gold that enabled Washington to pay his army and transport it to Yorktown. Not only were the soldiers without money, but they were absolutely destitute of supplies, without medicine for the fever-stricken soldiers, and without clothing or shoes. In addition to paying the wages of the soldiers in specie (the paper money of the government being at that time without value as a purchasing medium), this money bought them food, clothing, and munitions of war, and enabled Washington to compel the surrender at Yorktown.

TAKES LA FAYETTE TO FRANCE

On October 19, 1781, part of the British forces had surrendered in Virginia, and instead of being sent to destroy vessels of the enemy, Barry was again entrusted with the safe delivery of another envoy to France, her own distinguished son, the Marquis de la Fayette. The importance of La Fayette's mission to France was deemed by Washington to be greater than any service that could be rendered upon the field in America.

Washington, in his letter to Barry dated from Mount Vernon on November 15, 1781, wrote: "Respecting the operations of the next campaign, I do declare in one word that the advantages of it to America, and the honor and glory of it to the allied armies in these States, must depend absolutely upon the naval force which is employed in these seas at a time of its appearance next year. No land force can act decisively unless it is accompanied by a marine superiority, nor can more than negative advantages be expected without it. It follows, then, as certainly as that night succeeds day, that without a decisive naval force we can do nothing definite, and with it, everything honorable and glorious. A constant naval superiority would terminate the war speedily. Without it I do not know that it will ever be terminated honorably."

Robert Morris, chief of Department of Finance, in a letter of instructions to Barry, said: "I know your sense of duty and patriotism will lead you into all proper measures and exertions for the safety of your ship, for the success of her voyage and crew, and for the promotion of your country's interests."

With La Fayette safely landed back in France, Barry set sail for a homeward cruise. Robert Morris [1] wrote to Barry: "I do not fix your cruising ground because I expect you will know the most likely cruise and will be anxious to meet such events as will do honor to the American flag and promote the general interests."

CAPTURES TWO WAR-SHIPS IN SINGLE BATTLE

In a homeward cruise of the *Alliance* Barry fought and captured both the *Atalanta*, 16 guns, Captain Edwards, with 130 men, and the *Trepassy*, 14 guns, Captain Smith, with 80 men, engaging both vessels in a single battle. For more than an hour the *Alliance*, owing to unfavorable winds, fought under great disadvantage. Captain Barry was severely

[1] Morris was the leading shipping merchant of Philadelphia, and thoroughly informed about all the foreign sailing routes, as he was the owner of the largest number of ships sailing from that port to all parts of the world.—W. B. M.

wounded by a grape-shot through the shoulder. After a stubborn and manly resistance both the English vessels in the end were compelled to haul down their colors.

The *Alliance* was much damaged in this combat, and in all the sea "was anything less fit to float than Barry's vessel, except the enemy's ships, which he had reduced to a worse condition." Never, never was a more brilliant action fought "and never were ships in a worse condition after a fight."

Barry in the *Alliance* fought and captured in one engagement both the *Mars*, a heavy-armed vessel of 26 guns and 142 men, and the *Minerva*, 10 guns and 56 men.

Barry in the *Alliance* captured the British war-ship *Alert* (said to be a sister ship named after an armed vessel he captured at an earlier date in the Delaware River), with supplies, which he turned over to Washington for the American army.

BARRY CAPTURES NINE PRIZES ON ONE CRUISE

Barry made another cruise in the *Alliance* to France on an important mission, bringing into L'Orient four of the nine English vessels loaded with valuable cargoes, sending the other five prizes under prize-master's orders back to America.

The following are copies of some of the letters written by Barry to the Marquis de la Fayette and to our own Benjamin Franklin, commissioner and plenipotentiary to the French court, while Barry was with his ship, the *Alliance*, in port at L'Orient, France.

L'ORIENT, *28 Oct., 1782.*

SIR,—Permit me to acquaint your Lordship of my arrival in France, after a successful cruise. Wherein I took nine prizes, four of which I brought in here, the other five I sent back to America—a few days before I sailed I had the pleasure of seeing his Excellency, General Washington, who inquired very particular about your health. I am sorry to give you trouble, but it would lay me under particular obligations if you have anything new at court, or any expectations of peace soon, you would let me know it, as I sail in ten days on a cruise and perhaps may soon go to America. Be pleased to make my best respects to Count de Noailles.

(Signed)   JOHN BARRY.

To Marquis de la Fayette,
        Paris.

COMMODORE JOHN BARRY

L'Orient, *31 Oct.*, *1782*.

Sir,—I had the honor to write you a few days past. Wherein was a request that I fear will be too much trouble to you, however, as it is of material consequence to me to know if it is likely we shall have peace or not. I, therefore, flatter myself from a former desire to serve me, you will indulge me at this time, and, believe me, I shall ever hold it of the greatest favors conferred on,

(Signed)   John Barry.

His Excellency,
Marquis de la Fayette,
Paris.

L'Orient, *Nov. 17, 1782.*

Sir,—When I had the pleasure to receive your obliging letters I was very much indisposed with a fever which has confined me to my chambers this ten days. I am now, sir, just able to write a few lines to thank you for the information you was pleased to give. As for my going to Paris this time, it is out of my power, as the ship is ready to sail, only awaiting for my recovery, which I hope in a few days to be able to go on board. You say you are going to America. I envy the captain who is to take you. I wish I was in his place, but, although I am deprived of that happiness at present, I hope to have the pleasure to command the ship that conveys you to your native country, and then, sir, I will certainly pay a visit to Paris—and I hope to have the honor of seeing Lady La Fayette, whom I have not the pleasure to have ever seen. It was my brother that had that honor in Bordeaux, who is since lost at sea. Be pleased to give my best respects to Lady La Fayette and Count de Noailles, and believe me to be,

To Marquis de la Fayette. (Signed) J. BARRY.

BARRY'S LETTER TO BENJAMIN FRANKLIN

L'ORIENT, *31 Oct., 1782.*

SIR,—Having nothing to communicate to your Excellency of any consequence but my arrival here, and that Mr. Barclay[1] promised me he would announce. I, therefore, thought it would only be troubling your Excellency to write, as I was at that time in expectations of being at sea before an answer could come from Paris. Some necessaries being wanting to the ship has detained her longer than I expected.

Lieutenant Barney, of the Continental ship *General Washington*, being just arrived and who informs me he is immediately under your Excellency's particular orders—as she was built for the purpose of a cruiser,[2] and of course will be of little or no service on that head. I think you would render great service to the United States to order her out with the *Alliance*, who will sail in about ten days. I have the honor to be sir,

(Signed) JOHN BARRY.

His Excellency,
    Benj. Franklin, Esq.,
        Paris.

[1] United States Consul-General.—W. B. M.
[2] Not as a cargo carrier.—W. B. M.

FOUR PRIZE CAPTURES BRING $2,500,000

Regarding the four prize vessels which Barry brought into the port of L'Orient and already mentioned in Barry's letter to La Fayette of October 28, 1782 — it may be interesting to here mention that the sales of these four prize vessels with their cargoes, captured by Commodore Barry in the *Alliance*, and sold at public auction at a somewhat later period in the presence of the Judges of the Admiralty and King's Attorney in virtue of the condemnation of his Excellency, Benjamin Franklin, Esq., Plenipotentiary of the United States at Paris—amounted to the sum of $2,500,000 (gold).

Here we have an evidence of Barry's innate modesty, a characteristic which followed him throughout his entire career—so becoming a naval officer and a gentleman—who, after capturing nine prizes on this voyage, bringing four of the prizes into L'Orient, wrote to Franklin (see letter dated L'Orient, October 31, 1782, and heretofore made mention) at Paris, "Having nothing of importance to communicate of any consequence but my

31

arrival here (L'Orient), and that Mr. Barclay promised me he would announce.'' Evidently Barry was not afflicted with *cacoëthes scribendi*, or, as Juvenal expresses it, *insanabile scribendi cacœthes*—an insane desire for scribbling.

CAPTURES WAR-SHIP AND HER PRIZE

Barry, with the *Alliance*, on a cruise in foreign waters, captured an English war-vessel which had taken a Venetian ship as a prize, though Venice was at that time at peace with England; she was a valuable ship with a valuable cargo. Barry, with a prospect of prize money, could have claimed her as a prize to be disposed of in port and the results distributed among his crew. Barry, without hesitation, and acting entirely from the dictates of his own humanity and justice—ever zealous of the integrity and good name of his country above all considerations—denounced the English captain who had seized her as a pirate, set her free, and told the captain of the Venetian ship to go in peace.

There is every reason to believe that owing to this affair and actions of a similar nature taken by Barry in other cases, that a mutiny was planned among the crew on board ship, resulting from dissatisfaction (and also, no doubt, to the very irregular payment of wages by the government, owing to lack of funds, a not unusual condition prevailing throughout the Revolution) with these acts of justice on the part of their commander, that cost the crew so much of their prize prospects. Barry assembled the crew, addressed them from the quarter-deck, took their word that they would thereafter be loyal, and dismissed them to their duty, putting only the three ring-leaders in irons. When they reached home these ringleaders, instead of being executed (owing to Barry's pleas in their behalf before the court-martial for clemency) were permitted to enlist in the Continental forces.

FIRES THE LAST SHOT OF THE REVOLUTION

Barry fought the last battle and fired the last shot of the Revolution, when, on the *Alliance*, in March, 1783, he left Havana, convoying to our shores the Continental ship, *Luzerne*, both the ships carrying a large

amount of gold on Continental account. He
encountered the *Sybille* (followed by two
other English war-ships) which he almost
sank, and would have done so had not her
consorts hurried to her aid. That was the
last shot fired in the Revolution. This was
the last naval battle of the Revolutionary
War. Peace was declared April 11, 1783.

BARRY CRUISES ON ENGLAND'S SHORES

The "Log of the *Alliance*," kept by John
Kessler, is one of the most interesting, won-
derful, and admirably kept records of any ship
that ever floated, and for the purpose of this
review is too long to even outline the lists of
important achievements duly credited to that
vessel. Suffice, then, to state that it shows that
the *Alliance* under the command of Capt. John
Barry, who had selected for his regular cruising
grounds the broad Atlantic (then closely pa-
trolled by England's powerful sea force), sailed
from as far south as the West Indies along
or in close proximity to the regular chartered
lanes or sailing routes to L'Orient, France—a
harbor and friendly port in Brittany and in
close reach of the English Channel.

THE FRIGATE "ALLIANCE," UNDER JOHN BARRY'S COMMAND, IN BATTLE WITH THE ENGLISH WARSHIP "SYBILLE."

"LOG OF THE 'ALLIANCE'"

Barry, with the *Alliance*, made frequent cruises in foreign waters, in each of the years of 1781, 1782, and 1783. The record of the "Log" shows that in each and every cruise he made, Barry never failed to either "Take, destroy, or sink the enemy's ships." Those he captured in the waters of or near to England's shores he generally carried into friendly foreign ports, and other captures made in the waters of the broad Atlantic, that England's navy claimed as her own, he either brought direct or sent back under prize-masters' orders to America. The "Log" shows that Barry made many captures of British ships with valuable cargoes and carried them safely back to home ports.

Notwithstanding that these exploits are recorded in the "Log" in a plain, terse, and matter-of-fact way, with no attempt at embellishment, still it reads like a story of magic. Here we must bid farewell to that grand old ship, for the *Alliance* was shortly afterward sold.

COMMODORE JOHN BARRY

BARRY MAKES TRIP TO FOREIGN PORTS

Barry became restless, and, observing the hesitancy on the part of the shipping merchants to re-establish the foreign trade and commerce, he makes a trip on personal account to European ports and to China; that was one of the first trips that started trade with newly opened ports, and, after accomplishing his object, he returns to Philadelphia.

BARRY WANTS TO FIGHT BARBARY STATE PIRATES

Sir,—Finding that the government have partly determined to fit out some ships of war for the protection of our trade against the Algerians, I beg to offer myself for commander of the squadron conceiving myself competent, thereto assuring your Excellency that should I be honored with your approbation my utmost abilities and most unremitting attention shall be exerted for the good of my country and also to approve myself worthy of the high honor shown by your Excellency, to your obedient humble servant,

JOHN BARRY.

March 10, 1794.
His Excellency,
*   The President of the United States.*

COMMODORE JOHN BARRY

RATHER FIGHT THAN BUILD SHIPS

In the *American State Papers* on naval affairs, 1839, Vol. 1, the following copy appears of a "Report of progress made in building the (six) frigates authorized by an act of March 27, 1794."

PHILADELPHIA, *Dec. 18, 1794.*

To the Secretary of War:

SIR,—As soon as the Appropriation Act of Congress passed, 27 of March last, we observed a navy constructor was immediately employed, who has been steadily at work, drawing the draughts and making the necessary molds for building on the most eligible construction; all of which are now completed and sent on to the different yards where the ships are to be built. And we appeal to all those who have any knowledge of the science of naval architecture, of the great precaution that was absolutely necessary in laying the foundation of our infant navy, and the time it would consequently take to digest a good plan, to avoid errors, and fix dimensions, founded on the experience of all maritime Europe, as well as that of this country, so as to have ships the best adapted for the service of any that was ever built of the kind, which we are of an opinion has been happily effected, and that arrangements to commence the building of frigates has been judiciously made, and every pains taken to procure the most durable wood in the world—the live oak of Georgia; but the summer season having commenced before the appropriation was passed, at which time it is so very sickly in and about the islands of Georgia, that it was impossible to procure, and would have been both expensive and useless to have sent men thither to cut wood, if they could have been procured during the summer months. Early in October, however, a number of wood-cutters, that had previously engaged in Connecticut, arrived in Georgia, commenced their operations and have made such progress that one vessel has already arrived here with a full cargo; the master of which reports favorably as to the despatch of others that have been sent on by the Treasury Department for to take timber to different yards. The building of these frigates of live oak will certainly be a great saving to the United States, as we are well satisfied (accidents excepted) that their frames will be perfectly sound half a century hence, and it is very probable that they may continue so for a much longer period.[1] On the contrary, we are fully convinced, from experience, that if they be built of the best of white oak of America, their durability at the utmost would not exceed one-fourth of that time, and the expense of building and equipment is the same whether the ships are of the best or of the worst wood of this country; but had it been determined, in the

---

[1] Time has proven the correctness of Barry's judgment.— W. B. M.

first instance, to have built the ships of common oak, no greater progress could have been made, as there was no timber cut in any of the States; and to have cut it in the summer season when the sap was up, and build the ships of wood in that green state, they would have proved rotten and totally unfit for the public service in less than five years from the laying of their keels.

The undersigned, John Barry, has made a visit to Georgia, at the request of the Secretary of the Treasury, and is so well satisfied with the exertions of Mr. Morgan, who superintends the cutting and shipping the timber, that he has no doubt but the whole quantity will be cut between this and the month of February, and, if so, we are all of opinion that the ships may be built and completely equipped in the course of next year, as every preparation is made in the different yards, and for procuring all the material in the various branches, for going on with spirit and despatch.

It must be remembered that, in the first maritime countries in Europe where they have regular establishments for building ships of war, with dock-yards and large stocks of timber thereon, they seldom complete a frigate, of the magnitude of any of ours, in less than twelve months after she is raised, contract ships, built in the time of war, to answer the purpose of the moment, only excepted.

It would be highly gratifying to us, sir, who have thrown aside our former occupation, and the prospects that promise fair for increasing our fortunes, with a view of serving our country, and who have no desire of being mere sinecure officers, if we could at this moment embark and obey the commands of our country, in going in pursuit of a barbarous enemy [1] who now holds in chains and slavery so many of our unfortunate fellow-citizens, the relieving and restoring of which to the bosom of their families and friends are, with that of having an opportunity to chastise their cruel oppressors, objects of our greatest ambition, and which we anticipate with all the ardor of officers, of seamen, and of citizens. We, therefore, assure you, sir, that every exertion shall be made by us in our department to facilitate the building and equipment of the ships to which we have had the honor to be appointed commanders and superintendents.

(Signed)   JOHN BARRY.
RICHARD DALE.
THOMAS TRUXTON.

The following are the names of the six frigates then being built and referred to by Barry in his (the foregoing) letter to the Secretary of War, dated Philadelphia, December 18, 1794: the *United States*, 44 guns; the *Constitution*, 44 guns; the *President*, 44 guns; the *Constellation*, 38 guns; the *Chesapeake*, 38 guns; the *Congress*, 38 guns. The

[1] The pirates of the Barbary States.—W. B. M.

United States was the first ship that got into the water under the present organization of the navy. She was launched at Philadelphia on July 10, 1797, the command of which was given to Commodore John Barry, who superintended its construction.

Dennie, in the portfolio (1813), wrote: "His (Barry's) opinion was very influential in the adoption by the government of that excellent model for ships of war, the superiority of which over every other has been so strikingly proved, as to have extorted the acknowledgment even of our enemies."

In the *Journals of the Continental Congress*, page 1118, Vol. 12, 1778, the following resolution regarding an expedition against the province of the east end of Florida was adopted:

"Resolved, That Captain John Barry be and is hereby directed to take the command of all armed vessels employed on the intended expedition, and that this commission continue in force till the expiration of the invasion of East Florida (or until further orders of Congress). That he proceed with the utmost despatch to the State of Maryland in order

to expedite the galleys furnished by that
State, and proceed with them to Charleston,
in South Carolina."

COMMAND OF FLEET IN DELAWARE RIVER AND BAY

The following are abstracts taken by the
writer from some of the letters written by the
Marine Committee.

January 29, 1778.

To Captain John Barry:

Sir,—We have agreed to employ the *Pinnace* and
barges belonging to the Frigates, and the barge taken
up by Captain Jonah in the river Delaware on a cruise
under your command. We hereby empower you to
receive such war-like stores, provisions, and other
stores from the Navy Board, and to employ such
Continental naval officers not in actual service, and
to collect such a number of men as you shall think
necessary for officering, victualing, and equipping
said boats. We have directed the Navy Board to
furnish you with every necessary for equipping your
little fleet, and money to procure supplies for your
crews as occasion may require. You will give imme-
diate notice to General Washington of such stores
as you may capture—which are necessary for the
use of the army. We would have you sink or other-
wise destroy the hulls of all such vessels as you may

take, which cannot be removed to a place of safety. The vessels which you take and preserve must be libeled in the Court of Admiralty in the State into which they are carried. You will therefore employ some suitable attorney to libel for the same. Write to us frequently and particularly of your proceedings. Wishing you success.

March 11, 1778.

To Captain John Barry:

Sir,—We have received your letter of the 8th inst. and congratulate you on the successful commencement of your expedition and hope it will be attended with similar advantages to the public and glory to the gallant commander, brave officers and men concerned in it throughout the whole course. The good opinion you have of your prize schooner has determined us to purchase her for a cruiser; she is to be called the *Wasp.*

We observe that you have advised General Washington of your success, and expect that you have furnished him with inventories of what was on board your prizes. The prisoners you have taken and shall take you will deliver to the commander of the main army which may be most convenient to you.

We thank you for the early intelligence of your success—your well-known bravery and good conduct gives us strong hopes of hearing from you often on similar occasions. With best wishes for your success.

COMMODORE JOHN BARRY

March 26, 1778.

To Captain John Barry:

SIR,—We have received your letter of the 20th inst. covering an inventory of the goods lately captured. We think with you that the Bay (Delaware) will be the best for your meeting with success and hope you will use your utmost diligence in getting your small squadron down there. With regard to the prize goods you have captured, one-half, in our opinion, belongs to the continent. If it had fully appeared that the schooner *Alert* was a vessel of war and belonged to the Crown of Great Britain or was duly commissioned a privateer by his Britannic majesty and you had held, she would have been solely the property of the captors.

May 30, 1778.

To John Barry, Esquire:

SIR,—We having appointed you to command the Continental frigate *Raleigh*, now in Port of Boston in Massachusetts Bay, you are hereby directed to repair immediately to that place and there apply to the Honorable, the Commissioners of the Continental Navy Board, who will deliver up that frigate with all her appurtenances to your care.

August 24, 1778.

Captain John Barry, of the frigate "Raleigh":

SIR,—Immediately upon receipt of these orders you will commence on a cruise in company with the

COMMODORE JOHN BARRY

Continental brig, *Resistance*, Captain Bourke, between
Cape Henlopen and Occracock on the coast of North
Carolina, with a view to take certain armed vessels
fitted out by the Goodriches or any other of the
enemy's vessels that may be investing that coast.
As both the *Raleigh* and the *Resistance* may soon be
wanted to answer the purpose of a convoy, you are to
manage your cruise, also, that you may be ready to
receive future orders of this (the Marine) Committee.
For this purpose you are once a week to put into
Chesapeake Bay and call at the town of Hampton,
where you will find such orders lodged, and you are
to continue to cruise and call at Hampton in this
manner until you receive our instructions.

September 28, 1778.

Captain John Barry:

Sir,—We have received your favors of the 8th inst.
from Boston and are sorry to hear that so many of the
guns on board the *Raleigh* had burst in proving, but
we hope they will be speedily replaced and that you
will shortly receive this letter at Hampton, agreeable
to our former instructions which you acknowledge
having received.

As you represent the *Raleigh* to be exceeding foul,
and on that account unfit to cruise upon the coast,
we have concluded that you had best proceed to
Portsmouth in Virginia, where there is a Continental
shipyard, and on applying to our agents there, Messrs.
Maxwell and Loyal and Mr. David Stoddart, the

4   45

master-builders in the yard, they will furnish you with convenience to have her bottom cleaned. Should the frigate *Deane* and any other vessel be in company with you, you will order them to cruise while you are careening.

Nov. 6, 1779.

Captain John Barry:

Sir,—As you have been appointed to command a new Continental ship [1]—that is now on the stocks at Portsmouth in New Hampshire—you are hereby directed to repair to that place and hasten as much as may be in your power the completing of that ship which we are desirous to have done with all possible despatch. We have now communicated our desire on that head to the Honorable, the Navy Board at Boston, whom you will please to call in your way and receive such orders as they may think proper to give you.

Should Mr. Langdon and you agree that any alteration can be made in this ship that will render her more suitable than the present design, you will please to communicate your plan and a state of the ship which we will consider.

Nov. 20, 1779.

Captain John Barry:

Sir,—Agreeable to your desire, we have appointed Captain George Jerry Osborne to command the

---

[1] This ship was the largest to be built, and carried 74 guns —nearly double the number of any ship then building or that had heretofore been constructed.—W. B. M.

marines on board your ship, but as it will be a considerable time before there is occasion to raise his men, we have been so early in his appointment on the principle of his being useful in doing matters relative to the ship until that time, you will please to observe and employ him occasionally in such business as you may think proper.

The following letter from the Marine Committee, the last one here to be recorded, may call for a little explanation; owing to the lack of funds to complete this new ship of 74 guns and the considerable time required for its construction, Captain Barry was appointed to take command of the *Alliance*. When this new ship of 74 guns, was completed at a later period, Congress decided to present it to the French King, and this ship was sent to France.

Sept. 5, 1780.

Captain John Barry:

Sir,—The Board have appointed you to command of the Continental frigate *Alliance*, now in the port of Boston. You are therefore directed to repair thither as soon as possible, and when you arrive apply to the Honorable, the Commissioners of the Navy Board of that department, who will give you directions for your conduct in fitting and preparing the *Alliance* for sea with all possible despatch.

COMMODORE JOHN BARRY

An account of Barry's achievements in this vessel has already been mentioned.

(From original records at Washington, D. C.)

WAR DEPARTMENT, *June 5, 1794.*

SIR,—The President of the United States, by and with the advice and consent of the Senate, has appointed you to be a captain of one of the ships to be provided in pursuance of the act to provide a naval armament herein enclosed.

It is understood that the relative rank of the captains is to be in the following order: John Barry, Samuel Nicholson, Silas Talbot, Joshua Barney, Richard Dale, Thomas Truxton. You will inform me as soon as convenient whether you accept or decline the appointment. I am, sir, etc.,

HENRY KNOX,
Secretary of War.

To Captain Barry.

Barry's acceptance reads:

STRAWBERRY HILL, *June 6, 1794.*

SIR,—The honor done me in appointing me a commander in the navy of the United States is gratefully acknowledged and accepted by

Your most obedient,
Humble Serv't,

The Hon'ble Henry Knox,   JOHN BARRY.
Secretary of War.

COMMODORE JOHN BARRY

It may be well here to state that Barry had two residences—a town-house at 186 Chestnut Street, between Ninth and Tenth streets, Philadelphia, and a suburban home at and known as Strawberry Hill, located on the (then) outskirts of the city.

COMMODORE IN CHIEF OF NAVY

On the organization of the navy of the United States in 1794 Commodore Barry was appointed by President Washington the senior officer, and was directed to superintend the building of the frigate *United States*, 44 guns. On this vessel—the *United States*—Commodore Barry sailed, accompanied by the *Delaware*, Capt. Stephen Decatur, Sr., and cruised for the defense of American commerce in the West Indies, where he captured with his own ship the armed French privateers, *Sans Pareil* and *Jaloux*.

WASHINGTON HANDS BARRY COMMISSION NUMBER ONE

On February 22, 1797, the last birthday that Washington spent in the executive chambers, he issued the commission marked

Number One, which made John Barry the commander-in-chief of all the naval forces of the United States (to take rank from the 4th day of June, 1794), and which Washington took occasion to hand in person to Commodore Barry.

The gallant Captain Nicholson, then second in rank to Barry, wrote him from Boston on June 14, 1794: "Give me leave to congratulate you on your honorable appointment to the command of our navy. I make no doubt but it is to your satisfaction and all who wish well to his country."

Fenimore Cooper, in his *History of the Navy*, 1839, says: "that Barry's appointment met with general approbation, nor did anything ever occur to give the government reason to regret the selection."

FATHER OF THE NAVY

Dennie, of the *Portfolio*, in 1813—ten years after Barry's death—wrote: "Barry may justly be considered the Father of our Navy. His eminent service during our struggle for independence, the fidelity and ability with which he discharged the duties of the impor-

WASHINGTON PRESENTING THE COMMISSION AS SENIOR CAPTAIN
AND COMMANDER-IN-CHIEF OF THE U. S. NAVY TO JOHN BARRY

tant stations which he filled, give him lasting claim upon the gratitude of his country."

CAPTURES MORE FRENCH SHIPS

Toward the close of 1798 and 1799 Barry commanded a squadron of ten vessels, and took with his own ship, the *United States*, two armed vessels, the *L'Amour de la Patrie* and the *Tartuffe*. He continued to protect our merchantmen from depredations by the French.

Barry advised in a letter a separation between the Naval Department and the War Department—for by an act of April 26, 1798, the outlines of a plan and suggestions of Barry were practically carried out and adopted, and the organization which Barry suggested in that letter led to its original formation.

A number of the officers and midshipmen who sailed with Commodore Barry attained considerable distinction in the service—among the lieutenants, afterward commodores, Richard Dale, Barron, and Stewart; and among the midshipmen, Stephen Decatur, afterward commodore, and Richard Somers, who acquired much fame at Tripoli; also among the former lieutenants and midshipmen were Jacob Jones and William Montgomery Crane, both of whom rose to the rank of commodores.

LETTERS OF SECRETARY OF NAVY TO BARRY

The following are copies of letters from the Secretary of the Navy, Benj. Stoddert, to Barry, then on his ship, the *United States*, at Newport, Rhode Island.

NAVY DEPARTMENT, *Oct. 1, 1799.*

SIR,—I am honored with your letter of the 24th ult., by which I perceive that mine of the 20th had not then reached you. The reason there assigned for desiring you to continue at Newport, and not subject the ship to the delay which must unavoidably attend a journey to Philadelphia, will, I am sure, be satisfactory to yourself. I will, however, in addition, observe that your distinguished station at the head of our navy attracts the attention of all our officers, who observe your proceedings, and will in some measure form themselves by your example. In my last letter I informed you that it might still so happen that you might come on without any detention to the ship. I then had in view the particular desire of the President that you should carry our ministers to France, if they go. He has not, however, yet determined whether you are to be thus employed or not; from present appearances, I think it probable you

will not. You will, however, wait and hold yourself
in readiness to proceed either to Europe or the West
Indies at the shortest notice. I expect you may hear
your destination in course of the present week.
Anchors were ordered from New York and Boston on
the 27th of September.

The names of the officers of the navy with their
relative rank will be sent you with my next com-
munications.

(Signed)   BEN STODDERT.

To Capt. John Barry,
    Frigate, "United States,"
        Newport, R. I.

NAVY DEPARTMENT, *October 16, 1799.*

SIR,—The President having decided that the *United
States* shall carry our envoys to Europe, you will be
pleased to hold yourself in readiness to perform that
service by the 1st of November at farthest. Two
anchors have been ordered, one from New York and
one from Boston, of which you will take the choice,
and Messrs. Gibbs and Channing are directed to
furnish you with cable which is to be made con-
formable to your instruction, which you will be
pleased to attend to. Everything must be ready to
sail on the arrival of the Ministers.

(Signed)   BEN STODDERT.

To Capt. Barry,
    U. S. Frigate, Newport, R. I.

The following, a personal letter from the Secretary of the Navy to Commodore Barry, is here cited, not altogether to show the confidence reposed and the evidence of the kindliness of Barry's personality, than to present the touch of pathos in the human side of nature and the unconscious parental solicitude for the boys' welfare where the dangers of navigation and the ogre of grim-visaged war presents.

GEORGETOWN (D.C.), *24 Nov., 1800.*

DEAR SIR,—I send at length my son and young Boyd, the widow's son, to go on board the *United States.* I am afraid my boy is too careless and too thoughtless ever to make a good sailor. I am afraid, too, you will be too kind to him, and he has already been spoiled by too much indulgence. I hope you will not treat him too well, not excuse him from any of the duties performed by other boys of his age and standing. I shall be much obliged if you will order him to be very attentive to learn navigation from the chaplain. Capt. Dale, whom I expect to go in the same stage with these boys, promises to tell them what to buy for bedding and stores at Philadelphia— which will save you the trouble. But, perhaps, Dale may not go with them, and in that case they may stand in need of your directions.

The Congress have at last begun business; they seem to be better satisfied than was expected with

THE · PRESIDENT of

To *John*

I GEORGE WASHING

Registered

J. Stagg Jun

No One

and *Confidence in your Patriotism Valour*

and *Consent of the* SENATE, *appointed*

of the FRIGATE *called* UNITED ST

sand seven hundred and ninety four

Captain *and* Commander *by doing and*

strictly charge and require all Officers

your Orders as Captain and Comman

tions, from time to time as you shall re

superior Officer set over you according

THIS COMMISSION *to continue*

By the President

James McHenry

Secretary of War

FACSIMILE (REDUCED) OF B

NITED STATES *of* AMERICA

rry

President of the United States *reposing special Trust*
and Abilities have nominated, and by and with the Advice
tain in the NAVY *of the* UNITED STATES, *and Commander*
to take Rank from The Fourth day of June, one thou
therefore carefully and diligently to discharge the duty of
ing all manner of things thereunto belonging. And I
and Seamen under your command to be obedient to
nd you are to observe and follow such orders and direc
n the President of the United States, *or any*
les and discipline of War and the usuage of the Sea
luring the pleasure of the President of the United States.

under my hand at Philadelphia, the Twenty second
bruary, in the Year of our Lord one thousand seven
nd ninety seven; and of the Sovereignty and In
of the United States the Twenty first.

G Washington

COMMISSION, NUMBER ONE

their accommodations—but they certainly have a great deal to complain of. The navy appears very popular with them, and hope they will form a permanent system for progressing with it until we are able to rely on our own strength for protection.

(Signed)   BEN STODDERT.

To Commodore Barry,
          Philadelphia.

HEAD OF THE UNITED STATES NAVY

When our present navy was founded Barry was selected as the commander-in-chief by President Washington, who well knew his Revolutionary services as did his successor, President Adams, when operations against the French were ordered—and again Barry performed some notable exploits in the capture of French cruisers and privateers.

The very first record-book of our Navy Department has for its initial entry that a commission had been delivered to Barry to make seizures of French ravagers upon our country's commerce.

ANENT THE CAUSE OF THE FRENCH WAR

In the treaty formed by this government with France in the course of the Revolutionary

War, it was expressly stipulated that in return for the aid about to be given (which later on was so actively and generously given) this country would return the compliment should that country (France) engage in war with Great Britain or any other country. In the fourth year after this government was established we declined to comply with the terms of our treaty. As a result, France captured a number of our American ships and seized their cargoes in order that British commerce and supplies for the British might be cut off. Hence the war with France. In 1800, by mutual agreement, after considerable negotiations, the difference between the two nations was amicably adjusted.

JEFFERSON RETAINS BARRY AT HEAD OF THE NAVY

After the election of 1800, when President Jefferson proceeded to reduce the naval forces, nine captains only were retained; of these Barry was still the senior officer, commodore-in-chief, and head of the navy, holding that exalted position until his death, September 13, 1803, in his fifty-ninth year, in the city of Philadelphia.

Barry died childless, without issue either by his first or second wife.

To give sanction to the brief outlines of some of the important episodes in the naval career of Commodore John Barry that we hereinbefore have mentioned, I will take the liberty to here quote, in as brief a way as the occasion demands, from Dennie's biographical sketch of John Barry as it appeared in the *Portfolio*, July 13, 1813.

DENNIE'S BIOGRAPHICAL SKETCH OF BARRY

Joseph Dennie was a contemporary and fellow-citizen with Barry; he was a journalist of note, a graduate of Harvard in 1790; was admitted to the practice of law, but ultimately devoted himself to literature. He went to Philadelphia to become private secretary to Thomas Pickering, Secretary of State. He was editor of the *United States Gazette*, became editor of the *Portfolio* in Philadelphia in 1801 under the pen-name of "Oliver Old School." The following extracts are taken from what Dennie, in 1813, wrote.

"So many of the distinguished naval men of the present day commenced their career under Commodore Barry that he may justly be considered as the father of our navy. His (Barry's) memory is cherished and his character duly appreciated by those who were attached to him by habits of long-tried friendship, by those who shared with him the toils of war, and by those illustrious men who acquired, under his auspices, those habits of discipline and that exactness of naval science which, combined with and directing their dauntless intrepidity, have recently won unfailing laurels for their country.

"Commodore Barry served throughout the revolution with distinguished honor to himself and signal benefit to his country. Even during the interval of suspension from public employment, occasioned by chances of war, he was actively employed in annoying the commerce of the enemy in *letter of marque* vessels.

"Having espoused the cause of liberty from principle, he was attached to it with all the glow of patriotic enthusiasm; nothing could divert him from it nor damp his ardor.

"After the termination of hostilities Commodore Barry was retained in the public service, and, when it was deemed expedient to increase the naval establishment, he was appointed to superintend the building of the frigate *United States*, in Philadelphia, which was designed for his command. His opinion was very influential in the adoption by the government of that excellent model for ships of war, the superiority of which over every other has been so strikingly proved as to have extorted the acknowledgments even of our enemies.

"He (Barry) was eminently qualified for important stations which he filled. He possessed courage without rashness, a constancy of spirit which could not be subdued, a sound and intuitive judgment, consummate skill, a generosity of soul which tempered the sterner qualities of the hero, and recommended him no less attentive to the comfort and happiness of those the fortune of war threw into his power than he had been ambitious to conquer them. Having spent the greater part of a long life upon the ocean, he had seen every possible variety of service; he knew how to sympathize, therefore, with those who were subjected to his command; to this it was owing that, though a rigid disciplinarian, he always conciliated the attachment of his sailors. It is worthy of remark that no person who sailed with him as seaman, officer, or passenger has ever been heard to speak of him but with the most respectful gratitude, and in regard to his seamen, especially, with all the extravagance of eulogy. He never found any difficulty in making up a crew, and desertion from his ship was unknown.

"In the various relations of private life he was no less unexceptionable. As a citizen he was exemplary, as a friend sincere, as a husband tender and affectionate. The affability and frankness of his deportment ingratiated him with all who enjoyed the pleasure of his acquaintance; there was a native humor in his character which gave it a peculiar interest. His mansion was ever the residence of hospitality. Jealous of his own honor, he was never known to injure, designedly, the feelings of any one; and though possessed of a quickness of sensibility to the appearance of offence or impropriety, he never failed to express his regrets and make atonement for injuries prompted by an excess of feeling. He was just, charitable, and without disguise. As he was educated in the habits of religion,

STATUE OF COMMODORE JOHN BARRY, INDEPENDENCE SQUARE,
PHILADELPHIA, PA.

so he cultivated them through life; he enforced a strict observance of divine worship on board his ship, and scrupulously attended to the moral deportment of his crew; he had himself experienced the comforts of religion, and he died in its faith.

"After our differences with France were accommodated, he (Barry) retained the command of the *United States* until she laid up in ordinary, soon after the introduction of Mr. Jefferson to the executive chair.

"General Washington had the highest opinion of Barry's merits and entertained for him a sincere and lasting friendship.

"Commodore Barry did not survive the termination of his public services; though naturally of a strong and robust constitution, he had for many years been subject to an asthmatic affection, to which he fell a victim on the thirteenth day of September, 1803.

"Thus closed the life of one of the first patriots and best of men. Commodore Barry was in size above the ordinary stature; his person was graceful and commanding. His whole deportment was marked by dignity unmixed with ostentation, and his strongly marked countenance was expressive at once of the qualities of his mind and the virtues of his heart.

"The incidents adverted to in this sketch have been politely furnished me (Dennie) by two gentlemen now living who were intimately acquainted with Commodore Barry, and enjoyed his friendship from a very early period in life; one of whom sailed with him during the Revolution as a subordinate officer."

Dennie, in referring to Barry's exploit with four row-boats capturing the armed British schooner and four transports loaded with provisions and forage for the enemy's forces (the details of which we have already mentioned), says: "General Washington always spoke with great satisfaction of this enterprise. Indeed, he gave a public expression of thanks to the gallant Commodore Barry."

Dennie further writes:

"Having made several voyages to the West Indies in *letter of marque* vessels, he was afterward ordered to take command of a 74-gun ship building in New Hampshire. Congress having, however, concluded to present her to the King of France, the Commodore was appointed to the command of the frigate *Alliance*, 36 guns, then at Boston.   In February, 1781, she sailed for L'Orient, having on board Colonel Laurens and suite, on an important embassy to the French court.   He sailed from L'Orient early in 1781 on a cruise, and, having taken many prizes, on the 29th of May an event occurred that deserves notice.   On the preceding day two sails were discovered on the weather-bow, standing for the *Alliance;* after approaching near enough to be in sight during the night they hauled to the wind and stood on the same course with the *Alliance*. These vessels proved to be the *Atalanta* and the *Trepassy*.   From daylight to 3 P.M. a fierce engagement ensued.   When Captain Edwards, of the *Atalanta*, was conducted to Commodore Barry, who was confined to his cabin by a severe wound in his shoulder from a grape-shot, he presented his sword, which was immediately returned to him as a testimonial of the high opinion entertained for his bravery, the Commodore observing, at the same time, 'That he richly merited it, and that his King ought to give him a better ship.'

The *Alliance* had eleven killed and twenty-one wounded—among the latter several officers; her rigging and spars much shattered and severely damaged in her hull. The enemy had the same number killed and thirty wounded. We have been led into the detail of this victory, as it was considered at the time of its achievement a most brilliant exploit, and as an unequivocal evidence of the unconquerable firmness and intrepidity of the victor.

"In the fall of 1781 orders were received to fit the *Alliance* for taking the Marquis de la Fayette and Count de Noailles to France on public business. On the 25th of December she sailed from Boston with them on board.

"The *Alliance* left L'Orient in February, 1782, from which time she continued cruising with great success till March of the following year, when, shortly after leaving Havana, whither she had been ordered to bring to the United States a large quantity of specie, having in company the Continental ship *Luzerne*, of 20 guns, Captain Green, three frigates were discovered right ahead, two leagues distance. The American vessels were hove about; the enemy gave chase. The *Luzerne*, not sailing as fast as the *Alliance*, Commodore Barry ordered her captain to throw her guns overboard. A sail was then discovered on the weather-bow bearing down upon them: the *Alliance* hove out a signal which was answered; she proved to be a French ship of 50 guns. Relying upon her assistance, the Commodore concluded to bring the headmost of the enemy's ships to action; after inspiring his crew by an address, and going from gun to gun cautioning his men against too much haste and not to fire till ordered, he prepared for action. The enemy's ship was of equal size with the *Alliance*. A severe engagement followed; it was very soon perceptible that the *Alliance* was gaining the advantage; most of the enemy's guns were silenced and, after an action of fifty minutes, the enemy's ship was so severely damaged that she hoisted a signal of distress, when her two consorts joined her.

"The loss on board the *Alliance* was very trifling—three killed and eleven wounded. The enemy's loss was severe—thirty-seven killed and fifty wounded. The other English frigates were watching the movements of the

French ship, the captain of which, upon coming up with the *Alliance*, assigned as a reason for keeping aloof from the action that he was apprehensive the *Alliance* had been taken, and that the engagement was only a decoy.

"A respectable gentleman of this city (Philadelphia) to whose politeness we (Dennie) are indebted for important aid he had given us in the preparation of this article, was in the *Luzerne* at the time of the engagement. He says, 'Language cannot do justice to his (Barry's) gallantry.'

"A gentleman of distinguished naval reputation, when in the Mediterranean with the American squadron, was introduced to Capt. James Vashon, Esq., now vice-admiral of the red, the commander of the British frigate engaged with the *Alliance*. In the course of conversation he made particular inquiry after Captain Barry, related the circumstances of the action, and, with frankness of a generous enemy, confessed that he had never seen a ship so ably fought as the *Alliance;* that he had never before, to use his own words, 'received such a drubbing, and that he was indebted to the assistance of his consorts,'

66

"His public services were not limited by any customary rule of professional duty, but, without regard to personal expense, danger, or labor, his devotion to his country kept him constantly engaged in disinterested acts of public utility."

Let it be remembered that Barry was entrusted with special and hazardous voyages and especially instructed "not to go out of his way for a fight, but to keep clear of all vessels whatever" when carrying our commissioners and envoys to France, and when returning from foreign ports with valuable cargoes of money, arms, ammunition, food, clothing, and supplies for Washington's destitute soldiers, which enabled the patriots to prosecute a successful war. Indeed, Barry, in a letter addressed to Richard Henry Lee, the president of Congress, calls attention to these aforementioned instructions "which frequently ensured severe blows and fewer captures of prizes."

Here, then, are some of the important naval episodes duly credited to that American patriot, Commodore John Barry, and in full accord with the facts of history. Fenimore

Cooper wrote: "Commodore Barry as an officer and a man ranked very high. His affection to his adopted country was never doubted and was put to proof, as the British government bid high to detach him from its service during the Revolution."

NOTICES OF BARRY'S DEATH IN PUBLIC PRINT

The following notices of Commodore John Barry's death are taken from the newspapers published in his city (Philadelphia). In the *American* (Philadelphia) *Daily Advertiser* of Wednesday, September 14, 1803, is the announcement notice of his funeral.

"The friends of the late Commodore Barry are requested to attend his funeral this morning at ten o'clock from his late dwelling, No. 186 Chestnut Street, between Ninth and Tenth Streets."

"The members of the *Cincinnati* are particularly requested to attend the funeral of their deceased brother, Commodore John Barry, from his late dwelling, No. 186 Chestnut Street."

COMMODORE JOHN BARRY

In the *American Daily Advertiser* (Philadelphia) of September 15, 1803, the following editorial appears:

" When the death of this gallant officer was announced the numerous ornaments of his naval and domestic characters freshened in our recollection, and a blameless impulse was felt to pay his memory the homage of our gratitude and sincere respect; a tribute which the generous will be proud to echo, and which the ingenuous cannot disapprove.

" It may be needless to observe that Captain Barry espoused with ardor the cause of liberty early in the year 1775, or to say with what constancy of attachment and boldness of enterprise he supported her interest during the war; all who have read the details of that glorious struggle must be familiar with the name of Captain Barry, and view in him a patriot of true integrity and of undoubted bravery.

" His naval achievements would of themselves have reflected much honor on his memory, but these could not have endeared it

69

to his fellow-citizens had he wanted those
gentle and amiable virtues which embellish
the gentleman and ennoble the soldier. Nature, not less kind than Fortune, gave him a
heart which the carnage and desolation of war
could not harden into cruelty; and the tenor
of his naval career exhibits a proof that the art
of commanding does not consist in super-
cilious haughtiness, tyrannous insult, and
wanton severity.

"In the pleasing view which his life presents
we contemplate a trait worthy of admiration,
as well for its intrinsic excellence as for its
rare emergence in bustle and distraction of
war—a punctilious observance of the duties
of his religion. In the scope of his character,
then, we survey with pleasure a warm and
steady friend, a firm patriot, a mild and
humane commander, a valiant soldier, and a
good Christian, beloved by numerous friends,
honored by his compatriots, and respected by
all who knew him."

The following ode, "Lines on the Death of
Commodore Barry," by Michael Fortune, appears in the *American Daily Advertiser* (Philadelphia) September 24, 1803.

COMMODORE JOHN BARRY

Columbia's Friend! freed from this worldly coil,
Now rests (so heav'n ordains) from human toil:
A patriot firm thro' chequer'd life unblam'd,
A gallant Veteran for his prowess fam'd.
Beneath his Guidance, Lo! a Navy springs,
An infant Navy spreads its canvas wings.
A rising Nation's Weal, to shield, to save,
And guard her commerce on dang'rous wave.
Whoe'er the sage, his Character shall scan!
Must trace those Virtues that exalt the man.
The bold achievement and heroic deed,
To Honor's fame the laurel'd Brave that lead!

Long, for his Merits and unsully'd name,
(Dear to his friends and sanctify'd by fame)
His clay-cold Relicts shall his country mourn,
And with her tears bedew his hallow'd Urn.

Come cheering Hope, celestial Cherub come!
Say, that his Virtues soar beyond the Tomb;
Say, that with Mercy, in ethereal Guise,
His white-robed spirit climbs yon op'ning skies.

Philadelphia, Sept. 19, 1803.

EPITAPH FOR BARRY BY DR. RUSH

The eminent Dr. Benjamin Rush, of Philadelphia, who was contemporary with Barry,
asked the privilege of writing the epitaph of
Commodore John Barry, which was inscribed

upon the original tombstone placed over the grave in Saint Mary's Catholic churchyard at Philadelphia. Dr. Rush was active in the pre-Revolutionary movements and, as a member of the provincial conference of 1776, moved the resolution declaring the expediency of a declaration of independence—of which he was a signer. He was surgeon in the Pennsylvania navy, 1775–76, and in 1777 was appointed surgeon-general.

The following is a true copy of the epitaph in full, from the original manuscript written and signed by Dr. Rush.

"Let the patriot, the soldier, and Christian who visits these mansions of the dead, view this monument with respect. Beneath it are interred the remains of John Barry.

"He was born in the County of Wexford, in Ireland. But America was the object of his patriotism and the theater of his usefulness.

"In the Revolutionary War, which established the independence of the United States, he bore an early and active part as a captain in their navy, and afterward became its commander-in-chief.

"He fought often, and once bled in the

COMMODORE JOHN BARRY'S STATUE IN FRONT OF HISTORIC
INDEPENDENCE HALL, PHILADELPHIA, PA.

cause of freedom.   His habits of war did not lessen his virtues as a man, nor his piety as a Christian.

"He was gentle, kind, and just in private life, and was not less beloved by his family and friends than by his grateful country.   The number and objects of his charities will be known only at the time when his dust shall be reanimated and when He who sees in secret shall reward.

"In full belief in the doctrines of the Gospel, he peacefully resigned his soul into the arms of his Redeemer on September 13, 1803, in the 59th year of his age.

"His affectionate widow hath caused this marble to be erected to perpetuate his name, after the hearts of his fellow-citizens have ceased to be the living records of his public and private virtues."

As Dr. Rush was a fellow citizen, a warm personal friend of Barry, and a fellow-patriot in the cause of liberty and freedom, may I venture the suggestion (when Congress elects to have Barry's remains removed to a worthy and appropriate resting place) that the epitaph with certain modifications be reinscribed upon one of the marble slabs of a mausoleum, befitting a resting-place for the remains of that true American patriot, Commodore John Barry—the Father of the American Navy.

The present modest tomb where lie the remains of Commodore Barry, is located in a small graveyard which has been abandoned as a burial place and inaccessible to the public for more than one-half of a century, and presents a most gruesome and dilapidated appearance to the sight, and a scene of desolation that is hardly describable. On account of the disintegration and decay of the marble slabs of the old or original tomb, on which the Rush epitaph was inscribed, a new tomb was erected on the same site by friends some years ago; the epitaph, however, has been replaced by another inscription.

Incidentally, it may here be pertinent to state that Abbot, in his *History of the United States Blue-Jackets*, tells us, "That Lord Howe, then commander-in-chief of the British forces in America, offered the American (Barry) twenty thousand guineas—over one hundred thousand dollars in gold—and the command of a British frigate if he would detach himself from the American service," and Barry's answer was: *"Not for the value of the English navy and the command of it all could I be seduced from the cause of my country."*

My country, as it was, indeed, to Barry—whose zeal for his country's welfare was as unmistakable as it was unalloyed.

Sit tibi terra levis!

WASHINGTON, D. C.

THE END